EP Math 2
Printables

Easy Peasy

All-in-One
Homeschool

This book belongs to

This book was made for your convenience. It is available for printing from the Easy Peasy All-in-One Homeschool website. It contains all of the printables from Easy Peasy's Math 2 course. The instructions for each page are found in the online course.

Easy Peasy All-in-One Homeschool is a free online homeschool curriculum providing high quality education for children around the globe. It provides complete courses for pre-school through high school graduation. For EP's curriculum visit allinonehomeschool.com.

ISBN-13: 978-1533308207
ISBN-10: 1533308209

Contents

Date _____

My 201-300 Chart

For Lessons 6 through 10, use this chart to practice counting from 201 to 300.

For Lesson 6, write 201 in the first corner square. Fill in the 1s column. The next number is 211. The last number should be 291.

For Lesson 7, fill in the 2s column. Write 202 next to 201 and then fill in the rest of the column. The last number should be 292.

For Lesson 8, fill in the 3s column. The last number should be 293.

For Lesson 10, fill in the 10s column. The last number should be 300.

Addition up to 6 + 4

A. Practice addition up to 6 + 4.

6	5	2	6	3	6	4	6
+ 4	+ 3	+ 4	+ 3	+ 4	+ 2	+ 3	+ 4
☐	☐	☐	☐	☐	☐	☐	☐

B. Practice addition up to 4 + 6.

4	2	3	4	3	4	4	3
+ 6	+ 5	+ 3	+ 4	+ 5	+ 6	+ 5	+ 6
☐	☐	☐	☐	☐	☐	☐	☐

C. Connect the subtraction problems to their correct answers.

Addition & Comparison

A. Connect the problems to their correct answers.

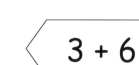

6 + 5	8	3 + 6
2 + 7	9	4 + 7
6 + 6	10	6 + 2
4 + 4	11	5 + 7
3 + 7	12	4 + 6

B. Compare the numbers with < (less than), > (greater than), or = (equal to).

360 ◯ 205	426 ◯ 500
265 ◯ 132	932 ◯ 239
657 ◯ 768	867 ◯ 724
336 ◯ 439	625 ◯ 635
874 ◯ 790	203 ◯ 523

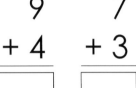

Date _____

Addition up to 9 + 4

A. Practice addition up to 9 + 4.

9	7	9	7	8	9	8	6
+ 4	+ 3	+ 3	+ 4	+ 3	+ 4	+ 4	+ 3
☐	☐	☐	☐	☐	☐	☐	☐

B. Practice addition up to 4 + 9.

4	3	4	3	4	3	3	4
+ 9	+ 6	+ 6	+ 8	+ 9	+ 9	+ 7	+ 8
☐	☐	☐	☐	☐	☐	☐	☐

C. Connect the problems to their correct answers.

4 + 6	**9**	8 + 3
7 + 2	**10**	5 + 7
6 + 7	**11**	4 + 5
6 + 5	**12**	3 + 7
4 + 8	**13**	4 + 9

Date _____

Tens and Ones

Write the correct number in each blank.

2 tens = **20**   6 tens = _____

3 tens = _____   7 tens = _____

4 tens = _____   8 tens = _____

5 tens = _____   9 tens = _____

2 tens + 5 ones = **25**   1 ten + 6 ones = **16**

4 tens + 3 ones = _____   3 tens + 8 ones = _____

8 tens + 1 one = _____   9 tens + 2 ones = _____

2 tens + 4 ones = _____   1 ten + 8 ones = _____

4 tens + 2 ones = _____   3 tens + 1 one = _____

8 tens + 9 ones = _____   9 tens + 5 ones = _____

5 tens + 8 ones = _____   6 tens + 4 ones = _____

3 tens + 2 ones = _____   7 tens + 3 ones = _____

This page is left blank for the cutting activity
on the next page.

Date _____

2D Shapes

Color and cut out the shapes to make a picture. Name each shape.

This page is left blank for the cutting activity
on the opposite side.

Date _____

Fact Families I

For Lessons 61 through 80, use these worksheets to fill in fact families.

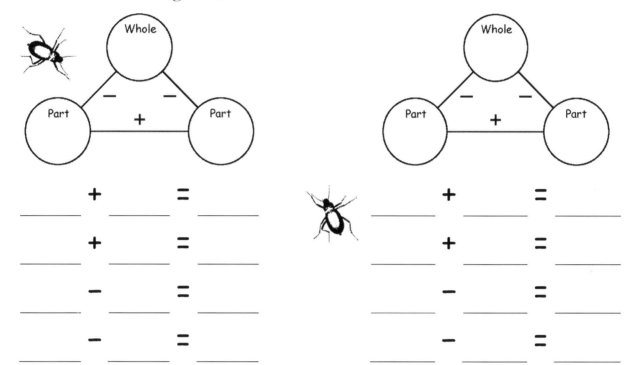

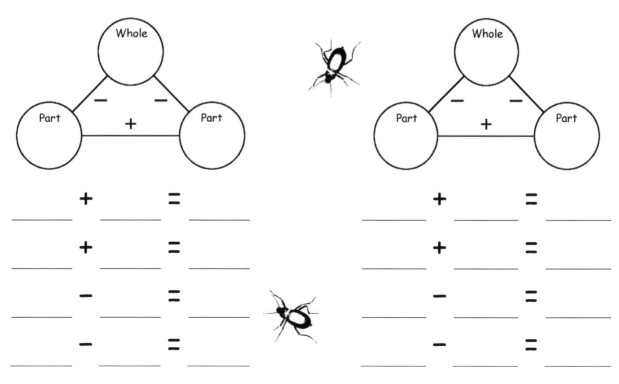

Date _____

Fact Families II

For Lessons 61 through 80, use these worksheets to fill in fact families.

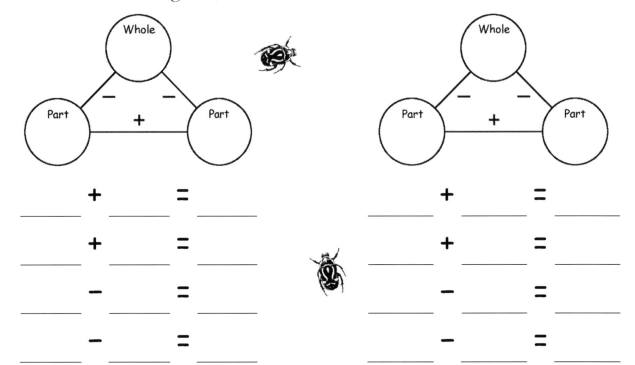

+ _____ = _____

+ _____ = _____

− _____ = _____

− _____ = _____

+ _____ = _____

+ _____ = _____

− _____ = _____

− _____ = _____

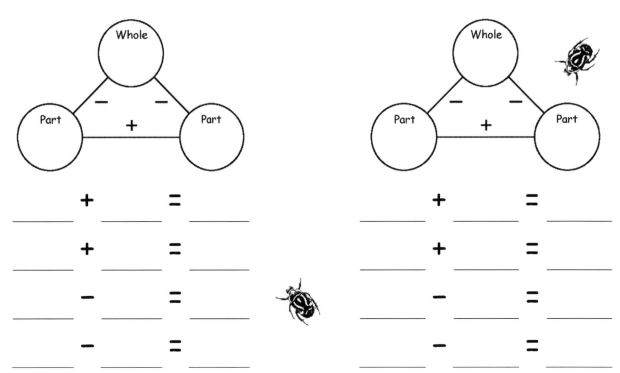

+ _____ = _____

+ _____ = _____

− _____ = _____

− _____ = _____

+ _____ = _____

+ _____ = _____

− _____ = _____

− _____ = _____

Fact Families III

For Lessons 61 through 80, use these worksheets to fill in fact families.

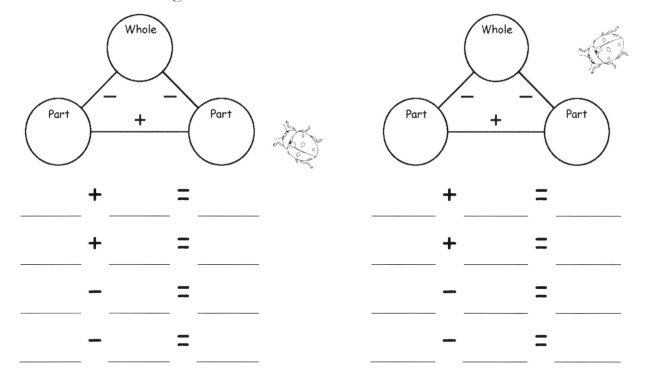

_____ + _____ = _____

_____ + _____ = _____

_____ − _____ = _____

_____ − _____ = _____

_____ + _____ = _____

_____ + _____ = _____

_____ − _____ = _____

_____ − _____ = _____

_____ + _____ = _____

_____ + _____ = _____

_____ − _____ = _____

_____ − _____ = _____

_____ + _____ = _____

_____ + _____ = _____

_____ − _____ = _____

_____ − _____ = _____

Date _____

Fact Families IV

For Lessons 61 through 80, use these worksheets to fill in fact families.

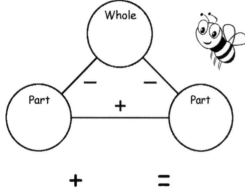

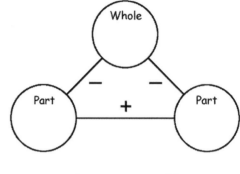

_____ + _____ = _____

_____ + _____ = _____

_____ − _____ = _____

_____ − _____ = _____

_____ + _____ = _____

_____ + _____ = _____

_____ − _____ = _____

_____ − _____ = _____

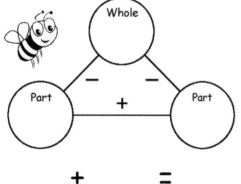

_____ + _____ = _____

_____ + _____ = _____

_____ − _____ = _____

_____ − _____ = _____

_____ + _____ = _____

_____ + _____ = _____

_____ − _____ = _____

_____ − _____ = _____

Date _____

Fact Families V

For Lessons 61 through 80, use these worksheets to fill in fact families.

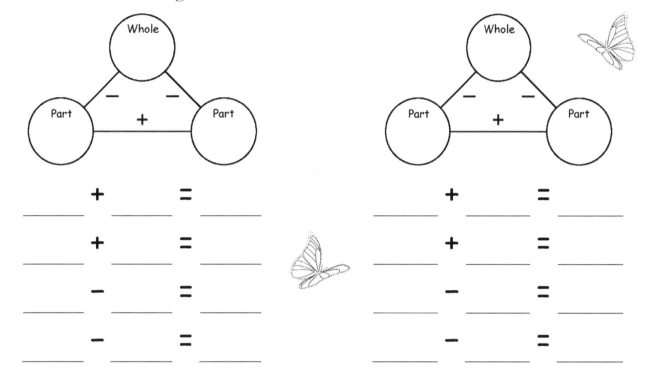

+ _____ = _____

+ _____ = _____

- _____ = _____

- _____ = _____

+ _____ = _____

+ _____ = _____

- _____ = _____

- _____ = _____

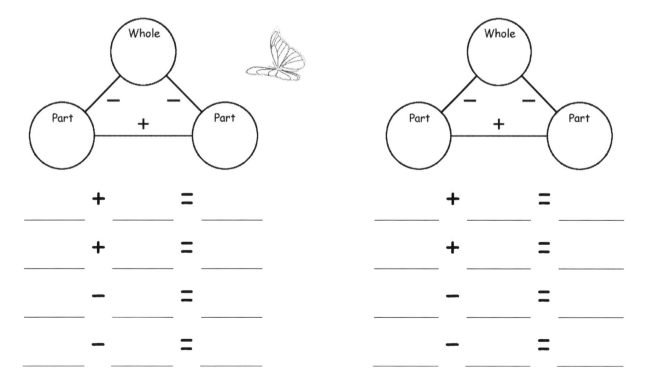

+ _____ = _____

+ _____ = _____

- _____ = _____

- _____ = _____

+ _____ = _____

+ _____ = _____

- _____ = _____

- _____ = _____

Date _____

Fact Families VI

For Lessons 61 through 80, use these worksheets to fill in fact families.

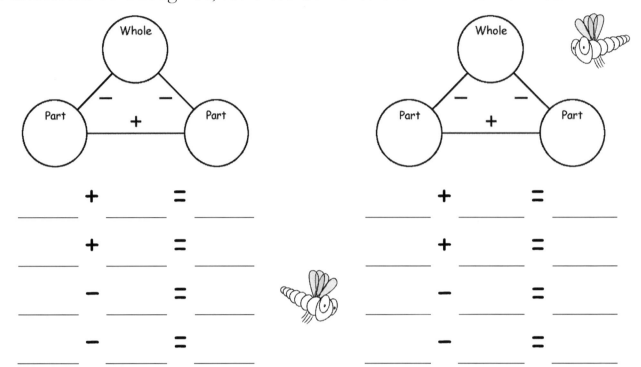

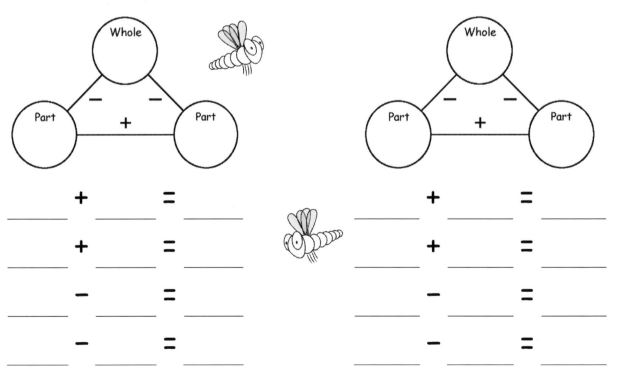

Date _____

Fact Families VII

For Lessons 61 through 80, use these worksheets to fill in fact families.

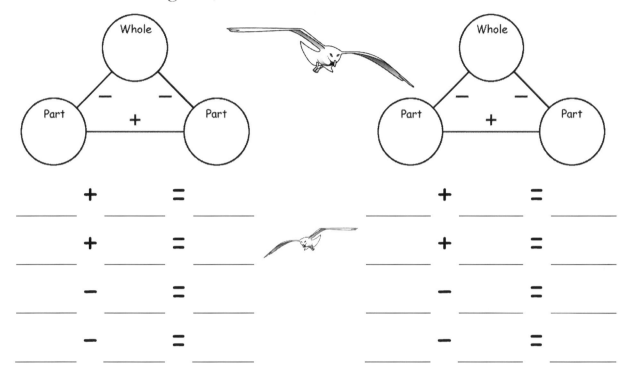

_____ **+** _____ **=** _____   _____ **+** _____ **=** _____

_____ **+** _____ **=** _____   _____ **+** _____ **=** _____

_____ **−** _____ **=** _____   _____ **−** _____ **=** _____

_____ **−** _____ **=** _____   _____ **−** _____ **=** _____

Subtraction Matching

Connect the problems to their correct answers.

| 8 - 4 | 7 - 5 | 11 - 5 | 6 - 3 | 10 - 5 |

| 10 - 4 | 8 - 5 | 9 - 4 | 8 - 6 | 7 - 3 |

| 8 - 3 | 6 - 4 | 5 - 2 | 9 - 3 | 10 - 6 |

Date _____

Subtraction Puzzles

Solve the subtraction problems. Use your **Fact Families** pages for help.

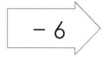

Date _____

Subtraction Crossword

Fill in the blanks. Use your **Fact Families** pages for help.

16	−	9	=		14	−	8	=		

$16 - 9 = \boxed{}$ $14 - 8 = \boxed{}$

$-$ $-$ $-$ $-$

13 $9 - 2 = \boxed{}$ 11 2

$-$ $=$ $=$ $=$ $-$ $=$

$5 - \boxed{} = \boxed{}$ $-$ $=$

$=$ $=$

$\boxed{} - 2 = \boxed{}$ $15 - \boxed{} = \boxed{}$

$-$

18 $11 - 4 = \boxed{}$ 8 10

$-$ $=$ $-$ $-$ $-$

$\boxed{} - 7 = \boxed{}$ $4 - 2 = \boxed{}$

$=$ $=$ $=$ $=$

$10 - \boxed{} = \boxed{}$

Date _____

3D Shapes I

Cut, fold and glue the edges to make a cube. Check the next page for more!

This page is left blank for the cutting activity
on the opposite side.

3D Shapes II

Cut, fold and glue the edges to make a pyramid and a tetrahedron.

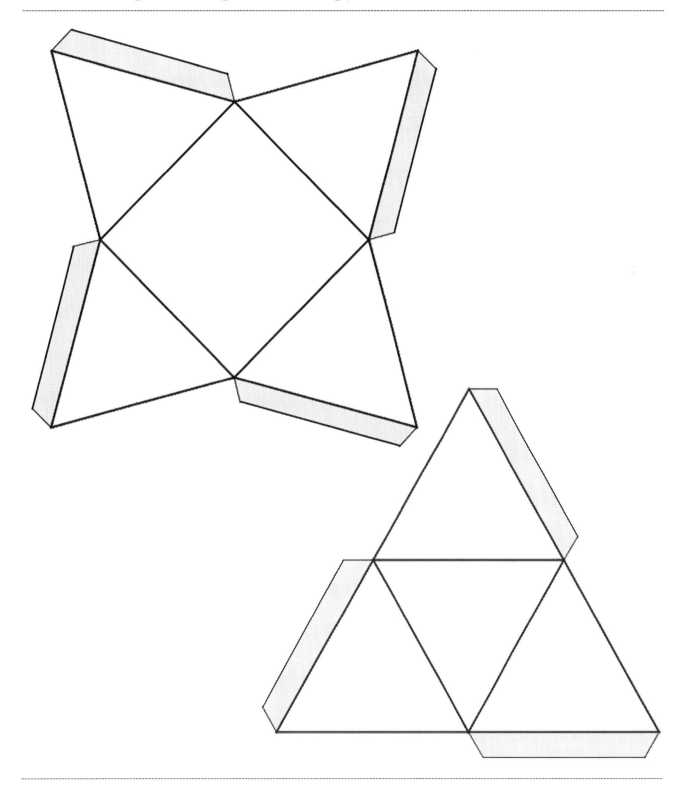

This page is left blank for the cutting activity
on the opposite side.

Date _____

Counting Coins

Use this hundreds chart to help you count coins.

1	2	3	4	5	6	7	8	9	10
11	12	13	14	15	16	17	18	19	20
21	22	23	24	25	26	27	28	29	30
31	32	33	34	35	36	37	38	39	40
41	42	43	44	45	46	47	48	49	50
51	52	53	54	55	56	57	58	59	60
61	62	63	64	65	66	67	68	69	70
71	72	73	74	75	76	77	78	79	80
81	82	83	84	85	86	87	88	89	90
91	92	93	94	95	96	97	98	99	100

A. Count 2 dimes and 3 pennies. How much money do you have? _____ ¢

B. Count 3 dimes and 3 nickels. How much money do you have? _____ ¢

C. Count 1 dime, 3 nickels, and 2 pennies. How much money do you have? _____ ¢

D. Count 2 dimes, 3 nickels, and 4 pennies. How much money do you have? _____ ¢

Date _____

Counting My Coins

Use this worksheet to practice counting your coins.

	How Many I Have	What They Are Worth

Date _____

Money Word Problems

Read each story problem. Write the answer.

Henry has 4 pennies in one hand and 3 dimes in the other hand. How much money does he have in all?

_____ ¢

Claire has 2 nickels. She finds 3 more nickels. How much money does she have in all?

_____ ¢

Derek has 1 nickel. Mia has 7 pennies. How much money do they have all together?

_____ ¢

Anne has 3 dimes. Paul has 5 pennies. Who has more money?

_____

  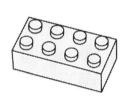  

Jacob bought a pear for 2 quarters and a candy for 8 pennies. How much money did Jacob spend in all?

_____ ¢

Orson had 20¢ until he spent 5 pennies on a LEGO block. How much money does Orson have now?

_____ ¢

Owen had 42¢ until he spent 2 dimes on an ice cream cone. How much money does Owen have now?

_____ ¢

Grace had 50¢ until she spent 1 quarter on glue. How much money does Grace have now?

_____ ¢

Date _____

Money Word Problems

Read each story problem. Write the answer.

What is the total of 25¢ and 40¢?   _____ ¢

What is 30¢ less than 64¢?   _____ ¢

Angela collects nickels and has 35¢ worth.
How many nickels does Angela have?   _____

Larry has 2 quarters and 4 dimes.
How much does he need to make a dollar?   _____ ¢

Mary had 65¢ but lost 20¢.
How much does she have left?   _____ ¢

Paul has 4 coins that add up to 17¢.
Which coins does Paul have?

_____ ¢   _____ ¢   _____ ¢   _____ ¢

80¢ is shared equally by four children.
How much money does each child get?   _____ ¢

How much money is four groups of coins with
1 dime and 2 nickels in each group?   _____ ¢

5 nickels and 3 pennies are shared equally by two
children. How much money does each child get?   _____ ¢

Date _____

Telling Time: To the 5 Minutes

Draw the hands on each clock face to show the time.

8:05

6:15

4:35

2:40

3:25

5:45

7:50

1:20

9:10

Time Passages: To the Hour

Write the time under the clock on the left. Read the word problem and write the new time and then draw the time on the blank clock.

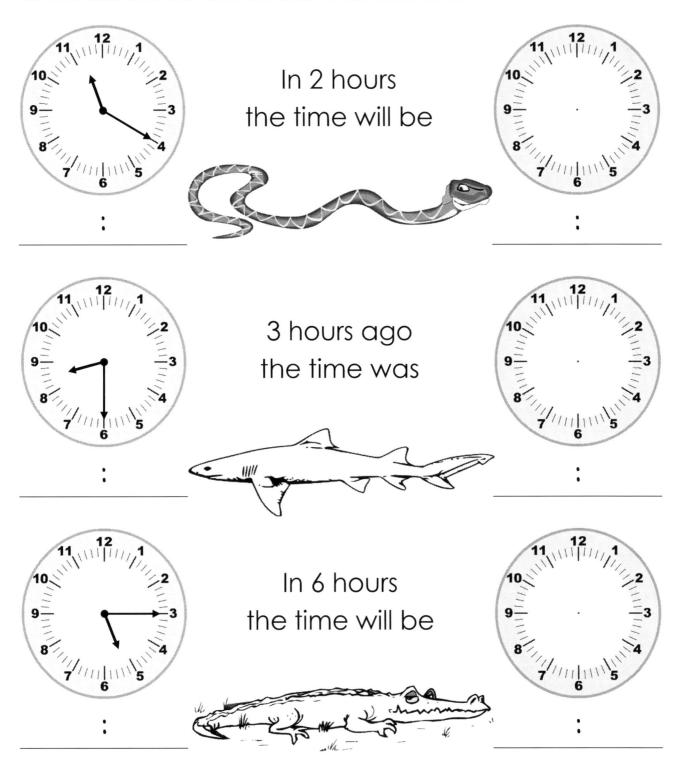

In 2 hours
the time will be

3 hours ago
the time was

In 6 hours
the time will be

Date _____

Telling Time: 5 Minutes Later

Sit down with someone who can tell time. Read the time on each clock. Say what time it is going to be in five minutes.

START!

END!

To play it as a game: Take turns. The player rolls the dice and moves forward to land on a clock. The player reads the time and tells what the time will be in five minutes. If the player is incorrect, move back two places. Play continues until all players have reached the end.

Date _____

Time Passages: To the Half Hour

Draw the clock hands to show the passage of time.

 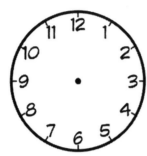  

What time will it be
in 4 hours 0 minutes?

What time will it be
in 8 hours 0 minutes?

 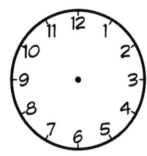  

What time will it be
in 2 hours 30 minutes?

What time will it be
in 3 hours 30 minutes?

   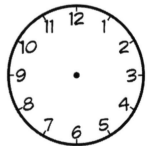

What time will it be
in 3 hours 30 minutes?

What time will it be
in 5 hours 0 minutes?

Date _____

Favorite Pets Bar Graph

Kim asked her friends to vote for their favorite pets. The tally chart shows their answers. Make a bar graph to represent the data from the tally chart.

Dog	Cat	Hamster	Fish	Snake
卌 III	卌 I	III	I	IIII

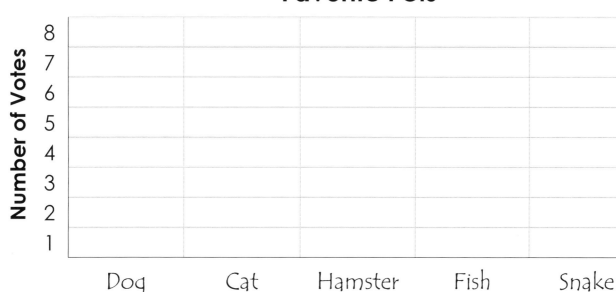

Favorite Pets

1. Which pet received the most number of votes? _____

2. Which pet received the least number of votes? _____

4. How many friends voted for snake? _____

5. How many friends voted all together? _____

6. How many more votes did dog receive than fish? _____

Date _____

My Bar Graph

Use this worksheet to make your own bar graph.

Title ⇨

⇧

Label ⇨

Date _____

Fractions of a Group

A. Circle the fraction that represents the shaded part of each group.

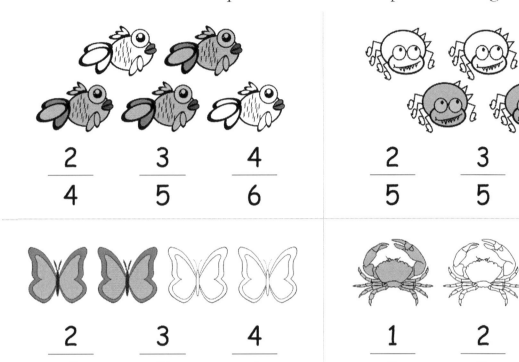

$$\frac{2}{4} \qquad \frac{3}{5} \qquad \frac{4}{6}$$

$$\frac{2}{5} \qquad \frac{3}{5} \qquad \frac{4}{5}$$

$$\frac{2}{4} \qquad \frac{3}{5} \qquad \frac{4}{6}$$

$$\frac{1}{3} \qquad \frac{2}{3} \qquad \frac{3}{3}$$

B. Write the fraction that represents the shaded part of each group.

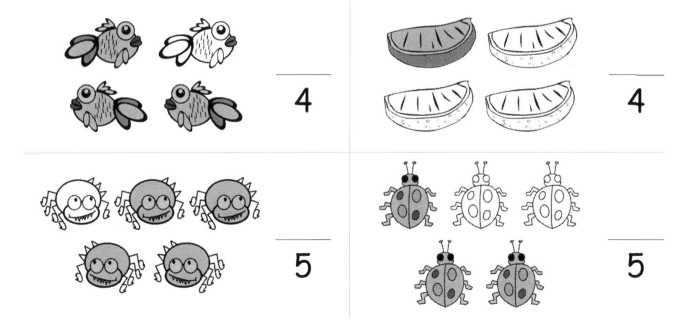

$$\frac{\quad}{4}$$

$$\frac{\quad}{4}$$

$$\frac{\quad}{5}$$

$$\frac{\quad}{5}$$

Date _____

Fractions in Words

Color in each shape to match the fraction in word form. Then write the fraction in number form to represent the colored part.

One half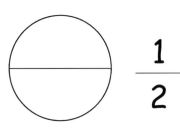

One third  __

One fourth 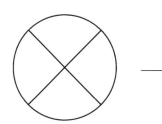 __

Two thirds 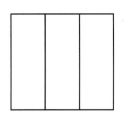 __

Three sixths 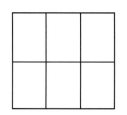 __

Five ninths 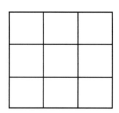 __

Two sixths 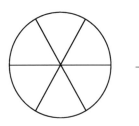 __

Three eighths 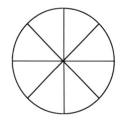 __

Six tenths 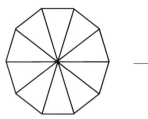 __

Three fifths 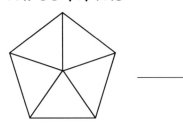 __

Four sixths  __

Fractions in Words

Match each picture with the fraction in number form and in word form.

$\dfrac{2}{3}$

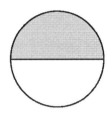

three eighths

$\dfrac{1}{2}$

two fourths

$\dfrac{2}{4}$

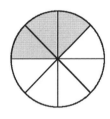

one half

$\dfrac{3}{5}$

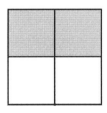

three fifths

$\dfrac{3}{8}$

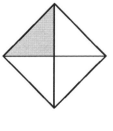

two thirds

$\dfrac{1}{4}$

one fourth

Date _____

Lemonade Bar Graph

Kyle had a lemonade stand. The tally chart shows how many cups of lemonade he sold each day. Make a bar graph to represent the data from the tally chart.

Monday	Tuesday	Wednesday	Thursday	Friday
⊬⊬ III	III	II	⊬⊬	⊬⊬

Lemonade Sales

Number of Cups

8
7
6
5
4
3
2
1

Monday　　Tuesday　Wednesday　Thursday　　Friday

Days

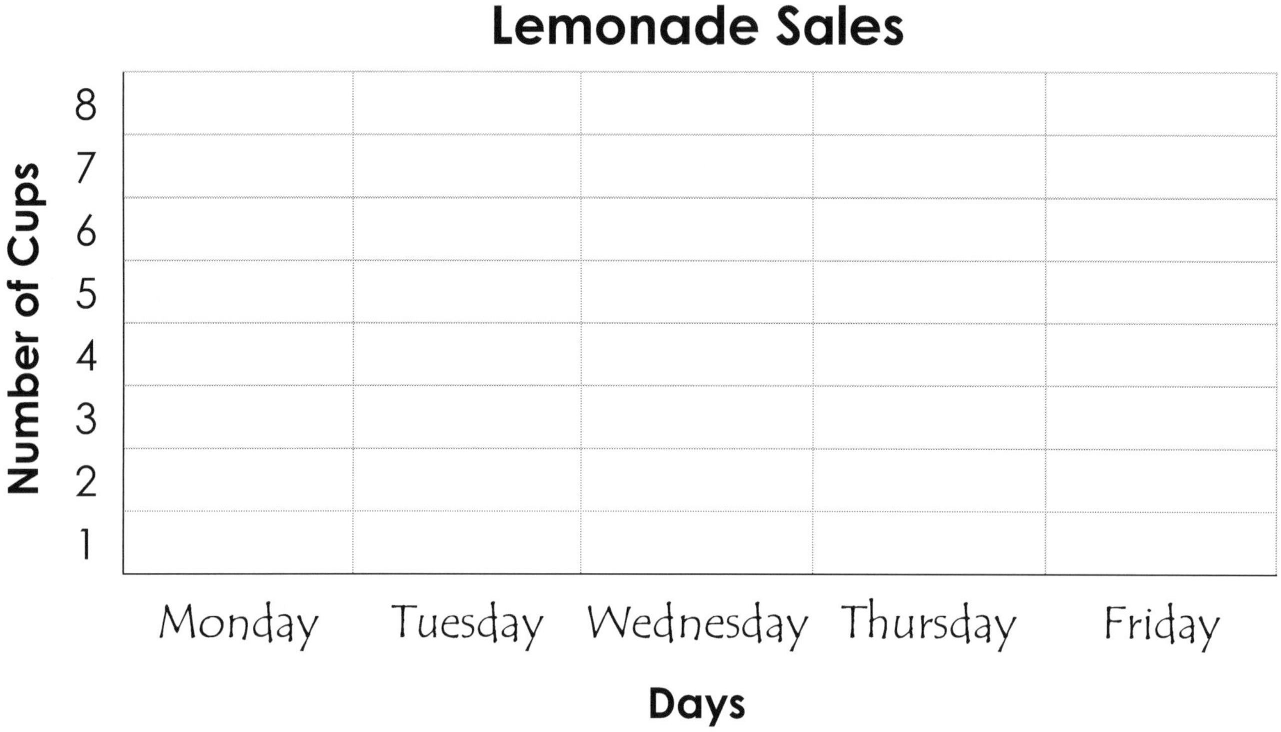

1. On which day did Kyle sell the most cups? _____

2. On which day did Kyle sell the fewest cups? _____

3. How many cups did Kyle sell on Tuesday and Friday? _____

4. How many cups did Kyle sell in total? _____

5. Kyle sold _____ more cups on Monday than on Wednesday.

6. Kyle sold the same number of cups on _____ and _____.

Date _____

Let's Review!

A. Solve the subtraction problems.

15 – 8 = _____   60 – 20 = _____

17 – 9 = _____   90 – 30 = _____

B. The puzzle pieces come from the 100s chart. Fill in the missing numbers.

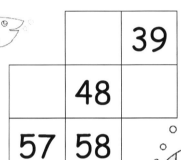

16	
26	27
	38

		39
	48	
57	58	

81	82		84
	92	93	

C. Read each question and fill in the blank.

✓ Is 57 closer to 50 or 60? _____

✓ November is the 11th month. March is the _____ month.

✓ Ella has thirteen stickers. Thomas has five stickers. Ella has _____ more stickers than Thomas.

D. Write the number that is ten less than:

_____ is ten less than 17

_____ is ten less than 30

_____ is ten less than 87

E. Write the sum or difference:

6 + 8 = _____

9 + 4 = _____

13 – 7 = _____

Let's Review!

A. Read each problem. Which and how many coins does each person have?

	25¢	10¢	5¢	1¢
Richard has three coins. The total amount is 12¢.				
Cooper has four coins. The total amount is 25¢.				
Gary has five coins. The total amount is 37¢				

B. Draw the next set of hearts to complete the pattern.

C. Draw the next set of blocks to complete the pattern.

  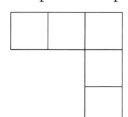

D. Read the story problem. What do you think?

There are goats, chickens, pigs, and dogs in the farmyard. You go out and count 22 legs. Which animals might you see?

Date _____

Tens and Ones

A. Separate tens and ones to complete each addition sentence.

12 = __10__ + _____   17 = _____ + __7__

24 = __20__ + _____   29 = _____ + __9__

37 = _____ + _____   46 = _____ + _____

53 = _____ + _____   61 = _____ + _____

B. Combine tens and ones to complete each addition sentence.

20 + 4 = _____   40 + 6 = _____

80 + 7 = _____   30 + 2 = _____

60 + 5 = _____   50 + 1 = _____

70 + 3 = _____

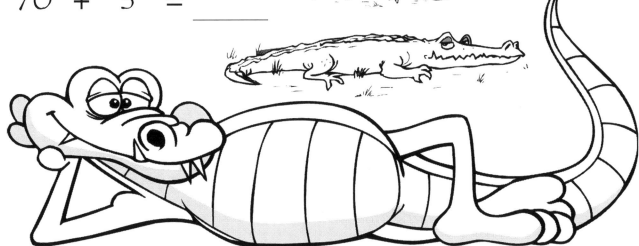

Date _____

Adding and Subtracting Tens

Solve the addition and subtraction problems.

3 tens	30	40	20	40	50
+ 5 tens	+ 50	+ 20	+ 30	+ 40	+ 20
8 tens	**80**				

3 tens	30	40	30	20	30
+ 4 tens	+ 40	+ 50	+ 30	+ 60	+ 20
tens					

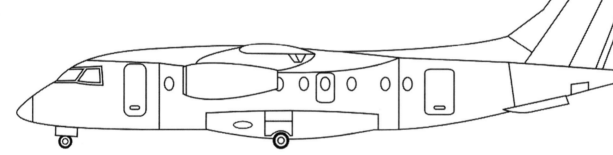

8 tens	80	70	90	60	80
− 4 tens	− 40	− 40	− 40	− 30	− 50
4 tens	**40**				

6 tens	60	90	70	80	90
− 4 tens	− 40	− 60	− 20	− 30	− 50
tens					

Date _____

Adding Tens

A. Count the number of blocks. Fill in the blanks.

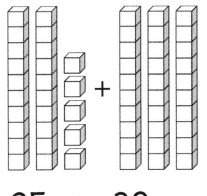  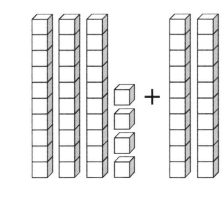

25 + 30 = _____   _____ + _____ = _____

B. Solve the addition problems.

10 + 10 = _____   20 + 10 = _____

15 + 10 = _____   35 + 10 = _____

11 + 10 = _____   22 + 10 = _____

18 + 10 = _____   29 + 10 = _____

42 + 10 = _____   37 + 10 = _____

71 + 10 = _____   66 + 10 = _____

20 + 20 = _____   40 + 20 = _____

50 + 20 = _____   50 + 30 = _____

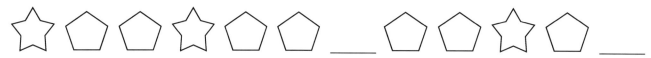
Let's Review!

A. Draw the missing shapes to complete the pattern.

☆ ⬠ ⬠ ☆ ⬠ ⬠ ___ ⬠ ⬠ ☆ ⬠ ___

B. Solve the addition problems. Fill in the blanks.

8 + ____ = 10   3 + ____ = 7

____ + 4 = 6   ____ + 2 = 9

C. Write the words as numbers.

seven	four	ten	six	zero	three

D. Write the time.

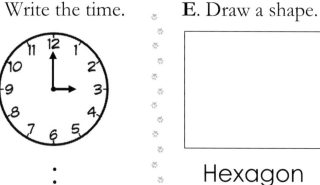

: _____

E. Draw a shape.

Hexagon

F. Solve the word problem.

Fifteen owls were sitting in a tree. Six flew away. How many were left?

_____

G. Use the graph to answer the questions.

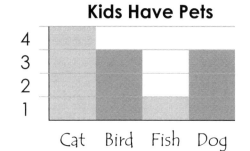

a. How many animals are there in all?

b. How many birds and dogs are there?

c. How many more cats are there than fish?

a. _____   b. _____   c. _____

Subtracting Tens

A. Count the number of blocks. Fill in the blanks.

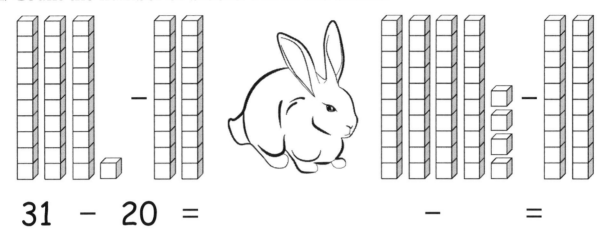

$$31 \ - \ 20 \ = \ \underline{\hspace{1cm}} \qquad\qquad \underline{\hspace{1cm}} \ - \ \underline{\hspace{1cm}} \ = \ \underline{\hspace{1cm}}$$

B. Solve the subtraction problems.

$10 \ - \ 10 \ = \ \underline{\hspace{1cm}}$ $20 \ - \ 10 \ = \ \underline{\hspace{1cm}}$

$25 \ - \ 10 \ = \ \underline{\hspace{1cm}}$ $35 \ - \ 10 \ = \ \underline{\hspace{1cm}}$

$30 \ - \ 10 \ = \ \underline{\hspace{1cm}}$ $32 \ - \ 10 \ = \ \underline{\hspace{1cm}}$

$78 \ - \ 10 \ = \ \underline{\hspace{1cm}}$ $79 \ - \ 10 \ = \ \underline{\hspace{1cm}}$

$42 \ - \ 10 \ = \ \underline{\hspace{1cm}}$ $37 \ - \ 10 \ = \ \underline{\hspace{1cm}}$

$71 \ - \ 10 \ = \ \underline{\hspace{1cm}}$ $66 \ - \ 10 \ = \ \underline{\hspace{1cm}}$

$20 \ - \ 20 \ = \ \underline{\hspace{1cm}}$ $40 \ - \ 20 \ = \ \underline{\hspace{1cm}}$

$50 \ - \ 20 \ = \ \underline{\hspace{1cm}}$ $50 \ - \ 30 \ = \ \underline{\hspace{1cm}}$

Date _____

Adding Tens

Solve the addition problems.

10 + 90 = _____

80 + 90 = _____

20 + 40 = _____

80 + 50 = _____

50 + 90 = _____

40 + 90 = _____

10 + 50 = _____

70 + 10 = _____

60 + 20 = _____

90 + 80 = _____

30 + 80 = _____

10 + 20 = _____

20 + 20 = _____

30 + 70 = _____

60 + 50 = _____

40 + 50 = _____

Date _____

Subtracting Tens

Solve the subtraction problems.

100 – 10 = _____   120 – 30 = _____

130 – 40 = _____   130 – 80 = _____

150 – 80 = _____   150 – 90 = _____

 80 – 60 = _____   170 – 90 = _____

140 – 70 = _____   160 – 80 = _____

170 – 90 = _____   110 – 70 = _____

120 – 40 = _____   140 – 60 = _____

150 – 60 = _____

140 – 90 = _____

Date _____

Subtracting Tens and Ones

A. Count the number of blocks. Fill in the blanks.

34 – 21 = _____   _____ – _____ = _____

B. Let's practice subtracting tens and ones.

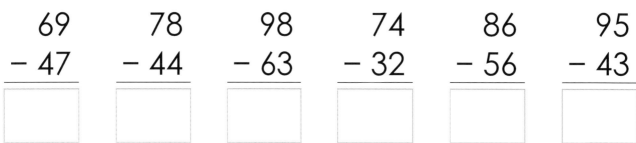

69	78	98	74	86	95
– 47	– 44	– 63	– 32	– 56	– 43

	87	19	48
	– 2	– 2	– 6

	59	47	36
	– 3	– 5	– 2

Date _____

Adding Tens and Ones

A. Count the number of blocks. Fill in the blanks.

46 + 2 = _____   _____ + _____ = _____

B. Let's practice adding tens and ones.

54	73	63	40	17	32
+ 5	+ 3	+ 4	+ 5	+ 2	+ 6

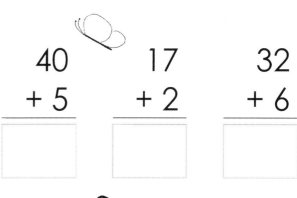

23	26	45
+ 75	+ 43	+ 42

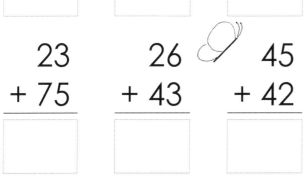

47	36	23
+ 21	+ 42	+ 22

Date _____

Adding and Subtracting Tens and Ones

A. Practice adding or subtracting ones.

62 + 7	25 − 3	35 + 2	98 − 4	36 − 4	43 + 5

57 − 3	48 − 2	15 + 4	91 + 7	79 − 6	73 + 3

B. Practice adding or subtracting tens and ones.

40 + 50	78 − 46	32 + 35	13 + 86	85 − 42	97 − 46

69 − 37	42 + 45	95 − 34	78 − 31	32 + 52	24 + 72

Adding 1 Digit with Regrouping

A. Count the number of blocks. Fill in the blanks.

37 + 4 = ____   ____ + ____ = ____

B. Solve the addition problems. Some of the problems may need regrouping.

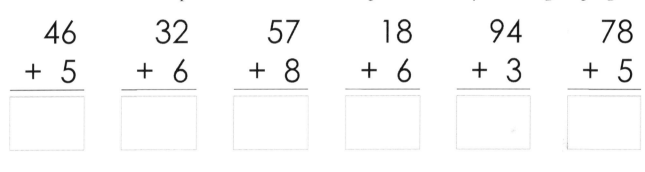

46	32	57	18	94	78
+ 5	+ 6	+ 8	+ 6	+ 3	+ 5

65	29	56	42	85	39
+ 2	+ 7	+ 7	+ 5	+ 7	+ 6

65	24	86
+ 9	+ 4	+ 6

Adding 2 Digits with Regrouping

A. Count the number of blocks. Fill in the blanks.

29 + 18 = _____   _____ + _____ = _____

B. Solve the addition problems. Some of the problems may need regrouping.

69	23	47	56	19	20
+ 23	+ 74	+ 25	+ 34	+ 75	+ 65

47	24	54	37	28	63
+ 49	+ 38	+ 24	+ 36	+ 56	+ 32

37	42	29
+ 43	+ 54	+ 49

Addition Word Problems

Solve each word problem. Write the equation and the answer.

Mark has ten baseball cards. Sam has eighteen baseball cards. How many baseball cards do they have in total?

10
+ 18

Bill had 42 marbles. Ethan gave Bill 25 marbles. How many marbles does Bill have now?

Owen found 16 ladybugs in the yard. Grace found 17 ladybugs. How many ladybugs did they find together?

Emma had twenty-eight dimes. Her mom gave her fifteen more dimes. How many dimes does Emma have now?

Larry read 34 pages of his storybook yesterday. He read 26 pages today. How many pages did Larry read in all?

Jenny picked 45 apples and Noah picked 39 apples from the apple tree. How many apples did they pick in total?

There were thirty-four books on the shelf. Orson placed eighteen more books. How many books are now there in all?

At the garden, Henry planted 16 flowers. Olivia planted 22 flowers. How many flowers did they plant in total?

2-Digit Addition

A. Count the number of blocks. Fill in the blanks.

28 + 17 = _____   _____ + _____ = _____

B. Solve the addition problems.

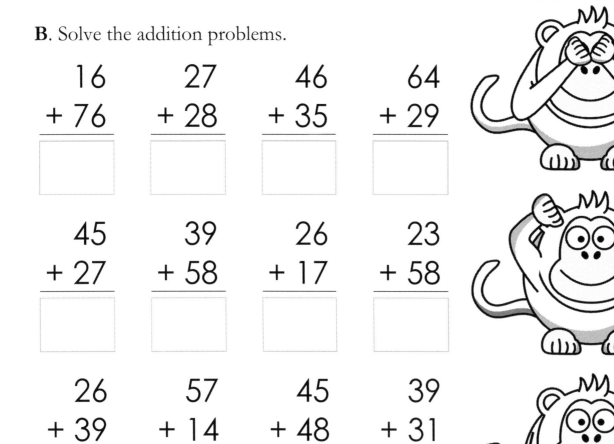

16	27	46	64
+ 76	+ 28	+ 35	+ 29

45	39	26	23
+ 27	+ 58	+ 17	+ 58

26	57	45	39
+ 39	+ 14	+ 48	+ 31

Subtraction Word Problems

Solve each word problem. Write your answer.

1. Mark had nine baseball cards but lost six of them. How many baseball cards does Mark have now?

   _____

2. Bill had seven marbles. Bill gave Ethan three marbles. How many marbles does Bill have now?

   _____

3. Mom made eight cookies. Owen ate four of them. How many cookies are left now?

   _____

4. Emma had seven nickels. Her sister borrowed two of her nickels. How many nickels does Emma have now?

   _____

5. Larry picked nine grapes and ate three of them. How many grapes does Larry have now?

   _____

6. At the orchard, Jenny picked eight apples and gave Noah five apples. How many apples does Jenny have now?

   _____

7. There were six books on the shelf. Orson took two books to read. How many books are left on the shelf?

   _____

8. Henry had eight crayons and broke two of them. How many unbroken crayons does Henry have now?

   _____

9. Seven children were wearing hats. Five children took their hats off. How many children were still wearing their hats?

   _____

10. Nine ducks were swimming in the pond. Four ducks flew away. How many ducks were still swimming in the pond?

   _____

Answer Key

Lesson 6+   Date _____

My 201-300 Chart

For Lessons 6 through 10, use this chart to practice counting from 201 to 300.

201	202	203							210
211	212	213							220
221	222	223							230
231	232	233							240
241	242	243							250
251	252	253							260
261	262	263							270
271	272	273							280
281	282	283							290
291	292	293							300

🐝 For Lesson 6, write 201 in the first corner square. Fill in the 1s column. The next number is 211. The last number should be 291.

🐝 For Lesson 7, fill in the 2s column. Write 202 next to 201 and then fill in the rest of the column. The last number should be 292.

🐝 For Lesson 8, fill in the 3s column. The last number should be 293.

🐝 For Lesson 10, fill in the 10s column. The last number should be 300.

Lesson 13   Date _____

Addition up to 6 + 4

A. Practice addition up to 6 + 4.

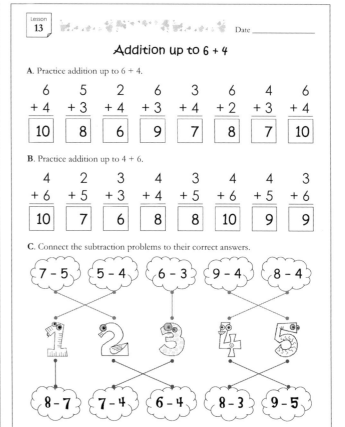

6	5	2	6	3	6	4	6
+4	+3	+4	+3	+4	+2	+3	+4
10	8	6	9	7	8	7	10

B. Practice addition up to 4 + 6.

4	2	3	4	3	4	4	3
+6	+5	+3	+4	+5	+6	+5	+6
10	7	6	8	8	10	9	9

C. Connect the subtraction problems to their correct answers.

7 – 5   5 – 4   6 – 3   9 – 4   8 – 4

1   2   3   4   5

8 – 7   7 – 4   6 – 4   8 – 3   9 – 5

Lesson 30   Date _____

Addition & Comparison

A. Connect the problems to their correct answers.

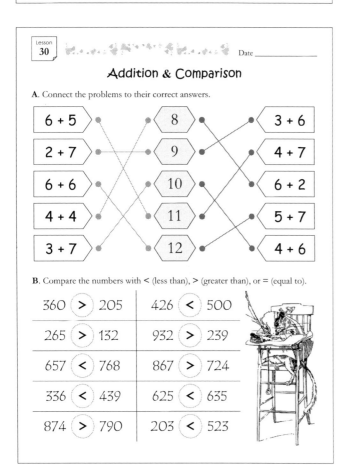

6 + 5   8   3 + 6
2 + 7   9   4 + 7
6 + 6   10   6 + 2
4 + 4   11   5 + 7
3 + 7   12   4 + 6

B. Compare the numbers with < (less than), > (greater than), or = (equal to).

360 > 205	426 < 500
265 > 132	932 > 239
657 < 768	867 > 724
336 < 439	625 < 635
874 > 790	203 < 523

Lesson 39   Date _____

Addition up to 9 + 4

A. Practice addition up to 9 + 4.

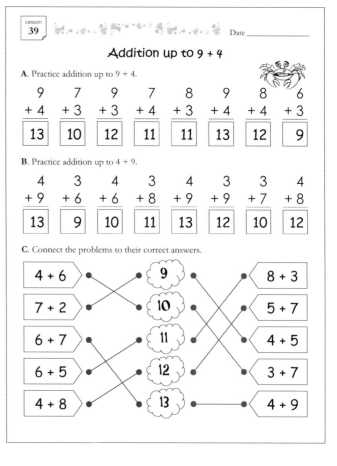

9	7	9	7	8	9	8	6
+4	+3	+3	+4	+3	+4	+4	+3
13	10	12	11	11	13	12	9

B. Practice addition up to 4 + 9.

4	3	4	3	4	3	3	4
+9	+6	+6	+8	+9	+9	+7	+8
13	9	10	11	13	12	10	12

C. Connect the problems to their correct answers.

4 + 6   9   8 + 3
7 + 2   10   5 + 7
6 + 7   11   4 + 5
6 + 5   12   3 + 7
4 + 8   13   4 + 9

Date _____

Tens and Ones

Write the correct number in each blank.

2 tens = __20__   6 tens = __60__

3 tens = __30__   7 tens = __70__

4 tens = __40__   8 tens = __80__

5 tens = __50__   9 tens = __90__

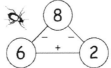

2 tens + 5 ones = __25__   1 ten + 6 ones = __16__

4 tens + 3 ones = __43__   3 tens + 8 ones = __38__

8 tens + 1 one = __81__   9 tens + 2 ones = __92__

2 tens + 4 ones = __24__   1 ten + 8 ones = __18__

4 tens + 2 ones = __42__   3 tens + 1 one = __31__

8 tens + 9 ones = __89__   9 tens + 5 ones = __95__

5 tens + 8 ones = __58__   6 tens + 4 ones = __64__

3 tens + 2 ones = __32__   7 tens + 3 ones = __73__

Date _____

Fact Families I

For Lessons 61 through 80, use these worksheets to fill in fact families.

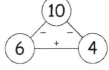

8 / 6 + 2

6 + 2 = 8
2 + 6 = 8
8 − 2 = 6
8 − 6 = 2

9 / 6 − 3

6 + 3 = 9
3 + 6 = 9
9 − 3 = 6
9 − 6 = 3

10 / 6 + 4

6 + 4 = 10
4 + 6 = 10
10 − 4 = 6
10 − 6 = 4

11 / 6 + 5

6 + 5 = 11
5 + 6 = 11
11 − 5 = 6
11 − 6 = 5

Date _____

Fact Families II

For Lessons 61 through 80, use these worksheets to fill in fact families.

13 / 6 + 7

6 + 7 = 13
7 + 6 = 13
13 − 7 = 6
13 − 6 = 7

14 / 6 + 8

6 + 8 = 14
8 + 6 = 14
14 − 8 = 6
14 − 6 = 8

15 / 6 + 9

6 + 9 = 15
9 + 6 = 15
15 − 9 = 6
15 − 6 = 9

9 / 7 + 2

7 + 2 = 9
2 + 7 = 9
9 − 2 = 7
9 − 7 = 2

Date _____

Fact Families III

For Lessons 61 through 80, use these worksheets to fill in fact families.

10 / 7 + 3

7 + 3 = 10
3 + 7 = 10
10 − 3 = 7
10 − 7 = 3

11 / 7 + 4

7 + 4 = 11
4 + 7 = 11
11 − 4 = 7
11 − 7 = 4

12 / 7 + 5

7 + 5 = 12
5 + 7 = 12
12 − 5 = 7
12 − 7 = 5

15 / 7 + 8

7 + 8 = 15
8 + 7 = 15
15 − 8 = 7
15 − 7 = 8

Date _____

Fact Families IV

For Lessons 61 through 80, use these worksheets to fill in fact families.

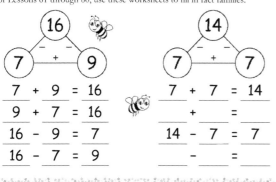

16
7 — + — 9

7 + 9 = 16
9 + 7 = 16
16 − 9 = 7
16 − 7 = 9

14
7 — + — 7

7 + 7 = 14
___ + ___ = ___
14 − 7 = 7
___ − ___ = ___

10
8 — + — 2

8 + 2 = 10
2 + 8 = 10
10 − 2 = 8
10 − 8 = 2

11
8 — + — 3

8 + 3 = 11
3 + 8 = 11
11 − 3 = 8
11 − 8 = 3

Date _____

Fact Families V

For Lessons 61 through 80, use these worksheets to fill in fact families.

12
8 — + — 4

8 + 4 = 12
4 + 8 = 12
12 − 4 = 8
12 − 8 = 4

13
8 — + — 5

8 + 5 = 13
5 + 8 = 13
13 − 5 = 8
13 − 8 = 5

11
9 — + — 2

9 + 2 = 11
2 + 9 = 11
11 − 2 = 9
11 − 9 = 2

12
9 — + — 3

9 + 3 = 12
3 + 9 = 12
12 − 3 = 9
12 − 9 = 3

Date _____

Fact Families VI

For Lessons 61 through 80, use these worksheets to fill in fact families.

13
9 — + — 4

9 + 4 = 13
4 + 9 = 13
13 − 4 = 9
13 − 9 = 4

14
9 — + — 5

9 + 5 = 14
5 + 9 = 14
14 − 5 = 9
14 − 9 = 5

16
8 — + — 8

8 + 8 = 16
___ + ___ = ___
16 − 8 = 8
___ − ___ = ___

17
9 — + — 8

9 + 8 = 17
8 + 9 = 17
17 − 8 = 9
17 − 9 = 8

Date _____

Fact Families VII

For Lessons 61 through 80, use these worksheets to fill in fact families.

12
6 — + — 6

6 + 6 = 12
___ + ___ = ___
12 − 6 = 6
___ − ___ = ___

18
9 — + — 9

9 + 9 = 18
___ + ___ = ___
18 − 9 = 9
___ − ___ = ___

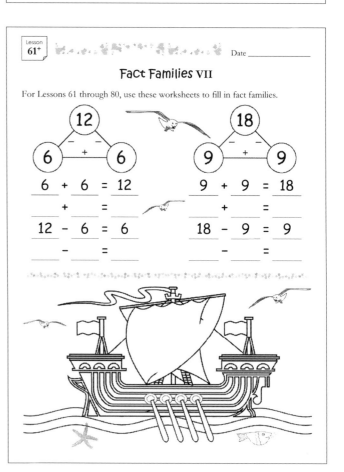

Date _____

Subtraction Matching

Connect the problems to their correct answers.

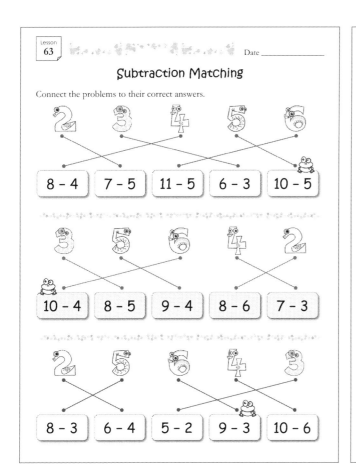

| 8 - 4 | 7 - 5 | 11 - 5 | 6 - 3 | 10 - 5 |

| 10 - 4 | 8 - 5 | 9 - 4 | 8 - 6 | 7 - 3 |

| 8 - 3 | 6 - 4 | 5 - 2 | 9 - 3 | 10 - 6 |

Date _____

Subtraction Puzzles

Solve the subtraction problems. Use your **Fact Families** pages for help.

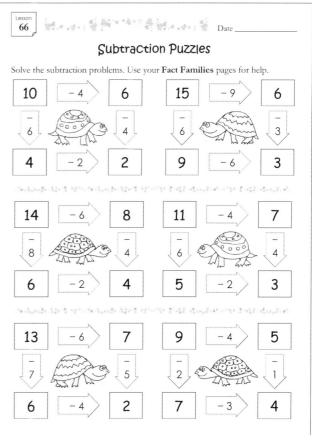

Date _____

Subtraction Crossword

Fill in the blanks. Use your **Fact Families** pages for help.

16	−	9	=	7		14	−	8	=	6
		−		−				−		
13		9	−	2	=	7		11		2
−		=		=		−		−		=
5	−	0	=	5		7	−	3	=	4
=								=		
8	−	2	=	6		15	−	8	=	7

18		11	−	4	=	7		8		10
−				=		−		−		−
9	−	7	=	2		4	−	2	=	2
=				=		=		=		=
9		10	−	7	=	3		6		8

Date _____

Counting Coins

Use this hundreds chart to help you count coins.

1	2	3	4	5	6	7	8	9	10
11	12	13	14	15	16	17	18	19	20
21	22	23	24	25	26	27	28	29	30
31	32	33	34	35	36	37	38	39	40
41	42	43	44	45	46	47	48	49	50
51	52	53	54	55	56	57	58	59	60
61	62	63	64	65	66	67	68	69	70
71	72	73	74	75	76	77	78	79	80
81	82	83	84	85	86	87	88	89	90
91	92	93	94	95	96	97	98	99	100

A. Count 2 dimes and 3 pennies. How much money do you have: 23 ¢

B. Count 3 dimes and 3 nickels. How much money do you have: 45 ¢

C. Count 1 dime, 3 nickels, and 2 pennies. How much money do you have: 27 ¢

D. Count 2 dimes, 3 nickels, and 4 pennies. How much money do you have: 39 ¢

Date _____

Money Word Problems

Read each story problem. Write the answer.

Henry has 4 pennies in one hand and 3 dimes in the other hand. How much money does he have in all?   **34** ¢

Claire has 2 nickels. She finds 3 more nickels. How much money does she have in all?   **25** ¢

Derek has 1 nickel. Mia has 7 pennies. How much money do they have all together?   **12** ¢

Anne has 3 dimes. Paul has 5 pennies. Who has more money?   **Anne**

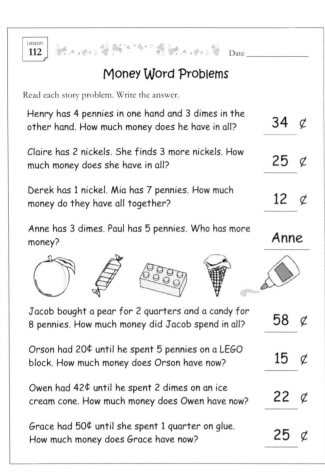

Jacob bought a pear for 2 quarters and a candy for 8 pennies. How much money did Jacob spend in all?   **58** ¢

Orson had 20¢ until he spent 5 pennies on a LEGO block. How much money does Orson have now?   **15** ¢

Owen had 42¢ until he spent 2 dimes on an ice cream cone. How much money does Owen have now?   **22** ¢

Grace had 50¢ until she spent 1 quarter on glue. How much money does Grace have now?   **25** ¢

Date _____

Money Word Problems

Read each story problem. Write the answer.

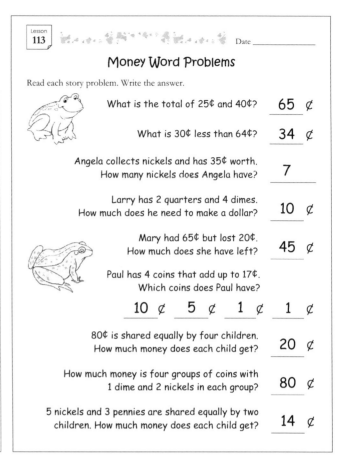

What is the total of 25¢ and 40¢?   **65** ¢

What is 30¢ less than 64¢?   **34** ¢

Angela collects nickels and has 35¢ worth. How many nickels does Angela have?   **7**

Larry has 2 quarters and 4 dimes. How much does he need to make a dollar?   **10** ¢

Mary had 65¢ but lost 20¢. How much does she have left?   **45** ¢

Paul has 4 coins that add up to 17¢. Which coins does Paul have?   **10** ¢   **5** ¢   **1** ¢   **1** ¢

80¢ is shared equally by four children. How much money does each child get?   **20** ¢

How much money is four groups of coins with 1 dime and 2 nickels in each group?   **80** ¢

5 nickels and 3 pennies are shared equally by two children. How much money does each child get?   **14** ¢

Date _____

Telling Time: To the 5 Minutes

Draw the hands on each clock face to show the time.

8:05   6:15   4:35

2:40   3:25   5:45

7:50   1:20   9:10

Date _____

Time Passages: To the Hour

Write the time under the clock on the left. Read the word problem and write the new time and then draw the time on the blank clock.

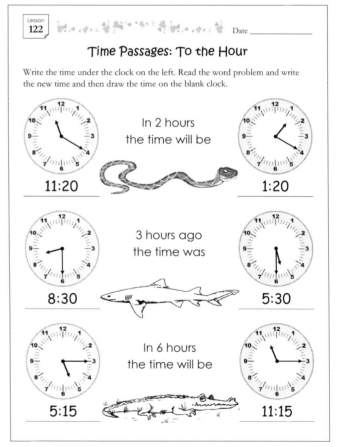

In 2 hours the time will be

11:20   1:20

3 hours ago the time was

8:30   5:30

In 6 hours the time will be

5:15   11:15

Telling Time: 5 Minutes Later

Sit down with someone who can tell time. Read the time on each clock. Say what time it is going to be in five minutes.

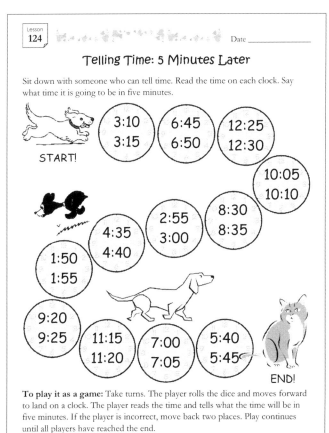

To play it as a game: Take turns. The player rolls the dice and moves forward to land on a clock. The player reads the time and tells what the time will be in five minutes. If the player is incorrect, move back two places. Play continues until all players have reached the end.

Time Passages: To the Half Hour

Draw the clock hands to show the passage of time.

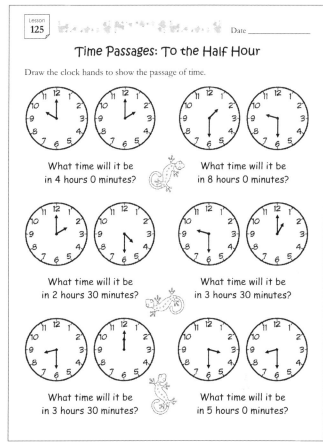

What time will it be in 4 hours 0 minutes?

What time will it be in 8 hours 0 minutes?

What time will it be in 2 hours 30 minutes?

What time will it be in 3 hours 30 minutes?

What time will it be in 3 hours 30 minutes?

What time will it be in 5 hours 0 minutes?

Favorite Pets Bar Graph

Kim asked her friends to vote for their favorite pets. The tally chart shows their answers. Make a bar graph to represent the data from the tally chart.

Dog	Cat	Hamster	Fish	Snake
卌 |||	卌		|||			||||

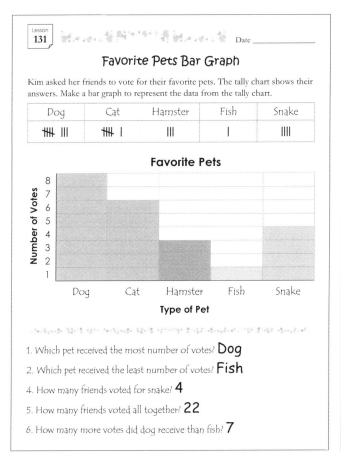

1. Which pet received the most number of votes? **Dog**

2. Which pet received the least number of votes? **Fish**

4. How many friends voted for snake? **4**

5. How many friends voted all together? **22**

6. How many more votes did dog receive than fish? **7**

Fractions of a Group

A. Circle the fraction that represents the shaded part of each group.

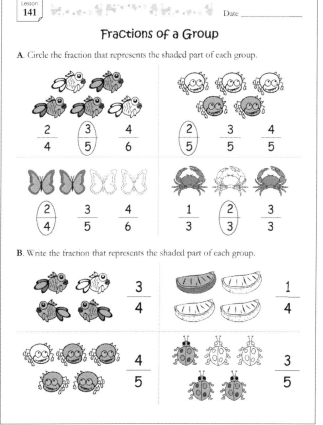

B. Write the fraction that represents the shaded part of each group.

Fractions in Words

Color in each shape to match the fraction in word form. Then write the fraction in number form to represent the colored part.

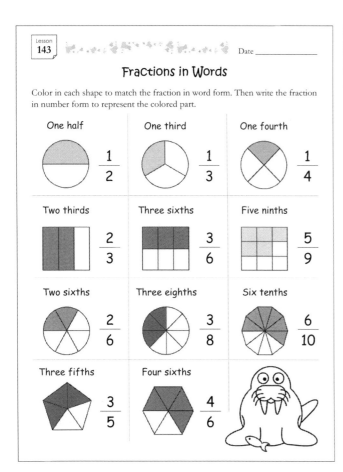

One half	One third	One fourth
$\frac{1}{2}$	$\frac{1}{3}$	$\frac{1}{4}$

Two thirds	Three sixths	Five ninths
$\frac{2}{3}$	$\frac{3}{6}$	$\frac{5}{9}$

Two sixths	Three eighths	Six tenths
$\frac{2}{6}$	$\frac{3}{8}$	$\frac{6}{10}$

Three fifths	Four sixths	
$\frac{3}{5}$	$\frac{4}{6}$	

Fractions in Words

Match each picture with the fraction in number form and in word form.

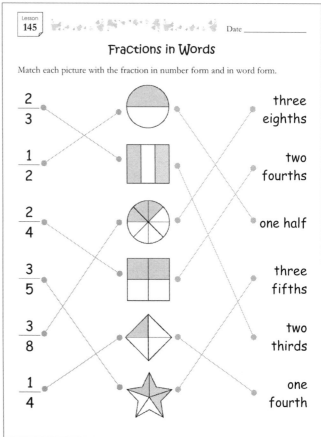

$\frac{2}{3}$ three eighths

$\frac{1}{2}$ two fourths

$\frac{2}{4}$ one half

$\frac{3}{5}$ three fifths

$\frac{3}{8}$ two thirds

$\frac{1}{4}$ one fourth

Lemonade Bar Graph

Kyle had a lemonade stand. The tally chart shows how many cups of lemonade he sold each day. Make a bar graph to represent the data from the tally chart.

Monday	Tuesday	Wednesday	Thursday	Friday
⊞⊞ III	III	II	⊞⊞	⊞⊞

Lemonade Sales

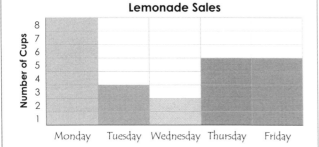

Days

1. On which day did Kyle sell the most cups? **Monday**

2. On which day did Kyle sell the fewest cups? **Wednesday**

3. How many cups did Kyle sell on Tuesday and Friday? **8**

4. How many cups did Kyle sell in total? **23**

5. Kyle sold **6** more cups on Monday than on Wednesday.

6. Kyle sold the same number of cups on **Thursday** and **Friday**.

Let's Review!

A. Solve the subtraction problems.

$15 - 8 = \underline{7}$ $60 - 20 = \underline{40}$

$17 - 9 = \underline{8}$ $90 - 30 = \underline{60}$

B. The puzzle pieces come from the 100s chart. Fill in the missing numbers.

16	17			38	39		72	73	74
26	27	28		47	48	49	81	82	83	84
	37	38		57	58		92	93	

C. Read each question and fill in the blank.

✓ Is 57 closer to 50 or 60? **60**

✓ November is the 11th month. March is the **3rd** month.

✓ Ella has **thirteen** stickers. Thomas has **five** stickers. Ella has **8** more stickers than Thomas.

D. Write the number that is ten less than:

$\underline{7}$ is ten less than 17

$\underline{20}$ is ten less than 30

$\underline{77}$ is ten less than 87

E. Write the sum or difference:

$6 + 8 = \underline{14}$

$9 + 4 = \underline{13}$

$13 - 7 = \underline{6}$

 Date _____

Let's Review!

A. Read each problem. Which and how many coins does each person have?

	25¢	10¢	5¢	1¢
Richard has three coins. The total amount is 12¢.	0	1	0	2
Cooper has four coins. The total amount is 25¢.	0	1	3	0
Gary has five coins. The total amount is 37¢	1	0	2	2

B. Draw the next set of hearts to complete the pattern.

C. Draw the next set of blocks to complete the pattern.

D. Read the story problem. What do you think?

There are goats, chickens, pigs, and dogs in the farmyard. You go out and count 22 legs. Which animals might you see?

The answer may vary, but you should see at least one chicken.

Lesson 160 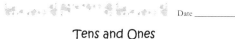 Date _____

Tens and Ones

A. Separate tens and ones to complete each addition sentence.

12 = __10__ + __2__   17 = __10__ + __7__

24 = __20__ + __4__   29 = __20__ + __9__

37 = __30__ + __7__   46 = __40__ + __6__

53 = __50__ + __3__   61 = __60__ + __1__

B. Combine tens and ones to complete each addition sentence.

20 + 4 = __24__   40 + 6 = __46__

80 + 7 = __87__   30 + 2 = __32__

60 + 5 = __65__   50 + 1 = __51__

70 + 3 = __73__

Lesson 162 Date _____

Adding and Subtracting Tens

Solve the addition and subtraction problems.

3 tens	30		40	20	40	50
+ 5 tens	+ 50		+ 20	+ 30	+ 40	+ 20
8 tens	80		60	50	80	70

3 tens	30		40	30	20	30
+ 4 tens	+ 40		+ 50	+ 30	+ 60	+ 20
7 tens	70		90	60	80	50

8 tens	80		70	90	60	80
− 4 tens	− 40		− 40	− 40	− 30	− 50
4 tens	40		30	50	30	30

6 tens	60		90	70	80	90
− 4 tens	− 40		− 60	− 20	− 30	− 50
2 tens	20		30	50	50	40

Lesson 166 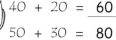 Date _____

Adding Tens

A. Count the number of blocks. Fill in the blanks.

  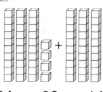

25 + 30 = __55__   34 + 30 = __64__

B. Solve the addition problems.

10 + 10 = __20__   20 + 10 = __30__

15 + 10 = __25__   35 + 10 = __45__

11 + 10 = __21__   22 + 10 = __32__

18 + 10 = __28__   29 + 10 = __39__

42 + 10 = __52__   37 + 10 = __47__

71 + 10 = __81__   66 + 10 = __76__

20 + 20 = __40__   40 + 20 = __60__

50 + 20 = __70__   50 + 30 = __80__

Let's Review!

A. Draw the missing shapes to complete the pattern.

B. Solve the addition problems. Fill in the blanks.

8 + _2_ = 10   3 + _4_ = 7

2 + _4_ = 6   _7_ + 2 = 9

C. Write the words as numbers.

seven	four	ten	six	zero	three
7	4	10	6	0	3

D. Write the time.

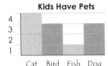

3:00

E. Draw a shape.

Hexagon

F. Solve the word problem.

Fifteen owls were sitting in a tree. Six flew away. How many were left?

9 owls

G. Use the graph to answer the questions.

Kids Have Pets

Cat Bird Fish Dog

a. How many animals are there in all?
b. How many birds and dogs are there?
c. How many more cats are there than fish?

a. _11_   b. _6_   c. _3_

Subtracting Tens

A. Count the number of blocks. Fill in the blanks.

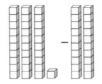

31 − 20 = 11   44 − 20 = 24

B. Solve the subtraction problems.

10 − 10 = _0_   20 − 10 = _10_

25 − 10 = _15_   35 − 10 = _25_

30 − 10 = _20_   32 − 10 = _22_

78 − 10 = _68_   79 − 10 = _69_

42 − 10 = _32_   37 − 10 = _27_

71 − 10 = _61_   66 − 10 = _56_

20 − 20 = _0_   40 − 20 = _20_

50 − 20 = _30_   50 − 30 = _20_

 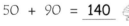
Adding Tens

Solve the addition problems.

10 + 90 = _100_

80 + 90 = _170_

20 + 40 = _60_

80 + 50 = _130_

50 + 90 = _140_

40 + 90 = _130_

10 + 50 = _60_

70 + 10 = _80_

60 + 20 = _80_

90 + 80 = _170_

30 + 80 = _110_

10 + 20 = _30_

20 + 20 = _40_

30 + 70 = _100_

60 + 50 = _110_

40 + 50 = _90_

Subtracting Tens

Solve the subtraction problems.

100 − 10 = _90_   120 − 30 = _90_

130 − 40 = _90_   130 − 80 = _50_

150 − 80 = _70_   150 − 90 = _60_

80 − 60 = _20_   170 − 90 = _80_

140 − 70 = _70_   160 − 80 = _80_

170 − 90 = _80_   110 − 70 = _40_

120 − 40 = _80_   140 − 60 = _80_

150 − 60 = _90_

140 − 90 = _50_

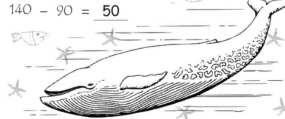

Lesson 171 Date _____

Subtracting Tens and Ones

A. Count the number of blocks. Fill in the blanks.

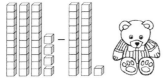 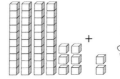

34 − 21 = 13   46 − 3 = 43

B. Let's practice subtracting tens and ones.

69	78	98	74	86	95
− 47	− 44	− 63	− 32	− 56	− 43
22	34	35	42	30	52

			87	19	48
			− 2	− 2	− 6
			85	17	42

			59	47	36
			− 3	− 5	− 2
			56	42	34

Lesson 172 Date _____

Adding Tens and Ones

A. Count the number of blocks. Fill in the blanks.

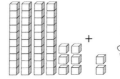

46 + 2 = 48   24 + 35 = 59

B. Let's practice adding tens and ones.

54	73	63	40	17	32
+ 5	+ 3	+ 4	+ 5	+ 2	+ 6
59	76	67	45	19	38

23	26	45
+ 75	+ 43	+ 42
98	69	87

47	36	23
+ 21	+ 42	+ 22
68	78	45

Lesson 173 Date _____

Adding and Subtracting Tens and Ones

A. Practice adding or subtracting ones.

62	25	35	98	36	43
+ 7	− 3	+ 2	− 4	− 4	+ 5
69	22	37	94	32	48

57	48	15	91	79	73
− 3	− 2	+ 4	+ 7	− 6	+ 3
54	46	19	98	73	76

B. Practice adding or subtracting tens and ones.

40	78	32	13	85	97
+ 50	− 46	+ 35	+ 86	− 42	− 46
90	32	67	99	43	51

69	42	95	78	32	24
− 37	+ 45	− 34	− 31	+ 52	+ 72
32	87	61	47	84	96

Lesson 175 Date _____

Adding 1 Digit with Regrouping

A. Count the number of blocks. Fill in the blanks.

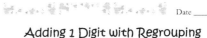 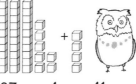 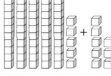

37 + 4 = 41   55 + 8 = 63

B. Solve the addition problems. Some of the problems may need regrouping.

46	32	57	18	94	78
+ 5	+ 6	+ 8	+ 6	+ 3	+ 5
51	38	65	24	97	83

65	29	56	42	85	39
+ 2	+ 7	+ 7	+ 5	+ 7	+ 6
67	36	63	47	92	45

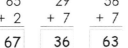

			65	24	86
			+ 9	+ 4	+ 6
			74	28	92

EP Math 2 Printables · 69

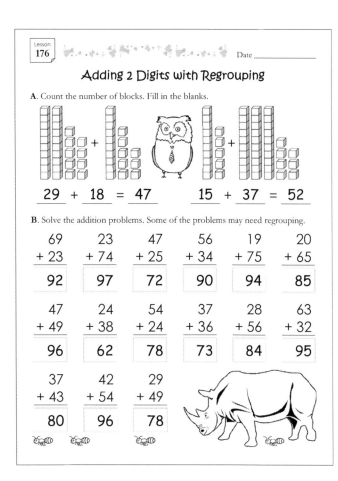

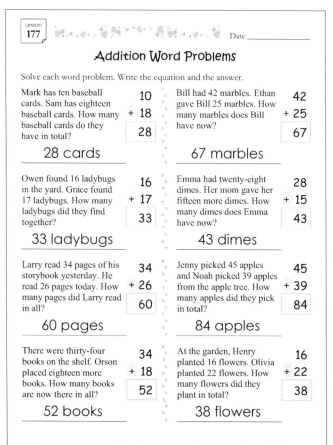

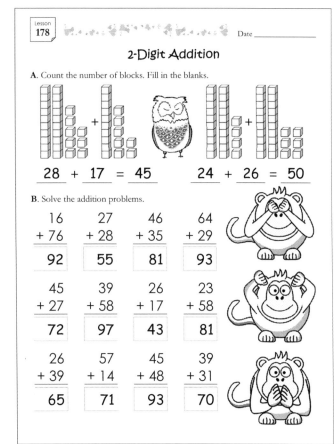

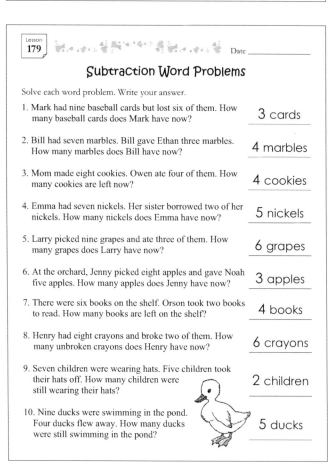

Lesson 176 — Adding 2 Digits with Regrouping

A. Count the number of blocks. Fill in the blanks.

29 + 18 = 47   15 + 37 = 52

B. Solve the addition problems. Some of the problems may need regrouping.

69	23	47	56	19	20
+ 23	+ 74	+ 25	+ 34	+ 75	+ 65
92	97	72	90	94	85

47	24	54	37	28	63
+ 49	+ 38	+ 24	+ 36	+ 56	+ 32
96	62	78	73	84	95

37	42	29
+ 43	+ 54	+ 49
80	96	78

Lesson 177 — Addition Word Problems

Solve each word problem. Write the equation and the answer.

Mark has ten baseball cards. Sam has eighteen baseball cards. How many baseball cards do they have in total?

10 + 18 = 28

28 cards

Bill had 42 marbles. Ethan gave Bill 25 marbles. How many marbles does Bill have now?

42 + 25 = 67

67 marbles

Owen found 16 ladybugs in the yard. Grace found 17 ladybugs. How many ladybugs did they find together?

16 + 17 = 33

33 ladybugs

Emma had twenty-eight dimes. Her mom gave her fifteen more dimes. How many dimes does Emma have now?

28 + 15 = 43

43 dimes

Larry read 34 pages of his storybook yesterday. He read 26 pages today. How many pages did Larry read in all?

34 + 26 = 60

60 pages

Jenny picked 45 apples and Noah picked 39 apples from the apple tree. How many apples did they pick in total?

45 + 39 = 84

84 apples

There were thirty-four books on the shelf. Orson placed eighteen more books. How many books are now there in all?

34 + 18 = 52

52 books

At the garden, Henry planted 16 flowers. Olivia planted 22 flowers. How many flowers did they plant in total?

16 + 22 = 38

38 flowers

Lesson 178 — 2-Digit Addition

A. Count the number of blocks. Fill in the blanks.

28 + 17 = 45   24 + 26 = 50

B. Solve the addition problems.

16	27	46	64
+ 76	+ 28	+ 35	+ 29
92	55	81	93

45	39	26	23
+ 27	+ 58	+ 17	+ 58
72	97	43	81

26	57	45	39
+ 39	+ 14	+ 48	+ 31
65	71	93	70

Lesson 179 — Subtraction Word Problems

Solve each word problem. Write your answer.

1. Mark had nine baseball cards but lost six of them. How many baseball cards does Mark have now? — **3 cards**

2. Bill had seven marbles. Bill gave Ethan three marbles. How many marbles does Bill have now? — **4 marbles**

3. Mom made eight cookies. Owen ate four of them. How many cookies are left now? — **4 cookies**

4. Emma had seven nickels. Her sister borrowed two of her nickels. How many nickels does Emma have now? — **5 nickels**

5. Larry picked nine grapes and ate three of them. How many grapes does Larry have now? — **6 grapes**

6. At the orchard, Jenny picked eight apples and gave Noah five apples. How many apples does Jenny have now? — **3 apples**

7. There were six books on the shelf. Orson took two books to read. How many books are left on the shelf? — **4 books**

8. Henry had eight crayons and broke two of them. How many unbroken crayons does Henry have now? — **6 crayons**

9. Seven children were wearing hats. Five children took their hats off. How many children were still wearing their hats? — **2 children**

10. Nine ducks were swimming in the pond. Four ducks flew away. How many ducks were still swimming in the pond? — **5 ducks**

Made in the USA
Columbia, SC
12 December 2020